Masonic Mnemonics

Memory Aids for Masonic Rituals

David Royal

Lewis Masonic

First published 2008
Reprinted 2009

ISBN 978 085318 292 4

All rights reserved. No part of this book may be reproduced or
transmitted in any form or by any means, electronic or mechanical,
including photocopying, recording or by any information storage and
retrieval system, without permission from the publisher in writing.

© David Royal 2008

Published by Lewis Masonic
an imprint of Ian Allan Publishing Ltd, Hersham, Surrey KT12 4RG.

Printed in England by Ian Allan Printing Ltd, Hersham KT12 4RG

Visit the Lewis Masonic website at www.lewismasonic.com

Masonic Mnemonics: Memory Aids for Masonic Ritual

I have always been in awe of those who would tell me of how they could "learn a page a day" or had the ability to "see the page" or "learn a section for next week". By the time I have learned my car registration, it's time to change the car.

For those of you who are like me, some form of memory aid is essential. The system presented here came about due to my inability to perform a ceremony in the Lodge as Master. I started my year after having attended LOI regularly and going through the Blue Book many, many times feeling that I would cope. Of course, I found that whereas I had always followed the ritual as performed by others, as Master nothing happened unless initiated by something I should have done or said. I was so disappointed by my performance that I was determined to do better.

In my work I am involved in training and writing training courses and as I looked at the ceremonies I thought to myself that the very last way I would write a training manual, for any task, would be to recommend to anyone to keep reading it over and over again.

Thus I constructed for my own use a training manual and this is how I produced what was considered a passable performance for the rest of my year (and, as it happened, the following year as well). My ritual will never be worthy of a silver Vesta case, but, once or twice, I have made a connection with the candidate; I have held their attention with every word. I have seen a tear in a man's eye and I know what I have said to them, was special, and will be recalled as a peculiar moment. To me that was worth a silver suitcase.

It is a fact that we come from man the hunter and for him it was essential for his survival that he remembered what he had seen. He needed to recognise both threats and opportunities quickly, as well as find his way home. This was before language, so the visual part of the brain is the most powerful at remembering. You can use this innate power of the mind to recall the ceremony as it unfolds before you. Learn the path of the candidate; understand the story and the context in which it is told. At each point in the ceremony the candidate will be in a unique position if you know why he is there it will trigger what you need to say. This system is often called 'Mind Mapping'. This will allow you to break up what seems to be an enormous chunk of unrelated words into smaller parts with each part a story in its own context.

There is symmetry in the ritual and many phrases are re-used in each of the degrees; understanding this can enable you to learn those common phrases and remember the difference for each degree.

It is also true of mankind that the art of story telling has always been revered and this was traditionally how history and information passed from generation to generation. The story told in the three degrees is worth listening to, regardless of how many times you may have heard it before.

I start with a question to which we should all know the answer; the answer to which tells us what we are about.

What is Freemasonry?

A peculiar system of morality, veiled in allegory, and illustrated by symbols.

Morality

- Standards of conduct that are accepted as right or proper.

Allegory

- A work in which the characters and events are to be understood as representing other things and symbolically expressing a deeper, often spiritual or moral meaning.
- The symbolic expression of a deeper meaning through a story or scene acted out by human, animal, or mythical characters.

Symbols

- Something that stands for or represents something else, especially an object representing an abstraction.

The rituals or ceremony of a Masonic Lodge which are to be learnt and repeated are in my view the most wonderful stories and are best approached as story tellers have done throughout mankind's existence. It requires more than just learning a few thousand words, without error! First, you must learn and understand the story. This story forms the skeleton or frame onto which you can hang and link the words. A good understanding of the context and content of those stories can only improve the telling of the same. We can further break this down in to its components, Context, Content and Detail.

Context

The Context for our purpose means the circumstances or events that form the setting within which the ceremony is to take place. In the larger sense, the initiation ceremony as a whole; and in the smaller scale the working tools of that degree. Each has a Context that can be learnt. This then forms a framework on which to hang the Detail.

Content

The Content deals with the meaning or message contained in the work as distinct from its appearance, form, or style. Story telling is not just about the spoken word; it requires body language, voice attenuation, passion and pauses. I think after- dinner speakers and stand-up comics call this timing.

The Detail

The Detail is all of the individual elements that together make up a whole. This will often be different for each Lodge as from my experience all Lodges are the same, each a little different! It may be the words are a little different from the Blue Book, or that where you are to stand or the order in which things are slightly different from the way that they are traditionally done in your Lodge. This is the province of your DC and Preceptor. This is a memory aid, not a ritual book. Be careful not to learn the ritual from this book; the ritual is incomplete and not strictly emulation. I recommend that you use the ritual book, with any modifications, as agreed within your Lodge. Mark the ritual book as appropriate or make notes on a piece of paper. My notes for the first degree would make little sense to anyone and the whole degree fills only two sides of A4.

Finally before we move on I apologise if anything I have chosen to aid my memory offends; this is not a book on Freemasonry but a memory aid to the ceremonies of Freemasonry. Any views I express are my own and serve to remind me of what I need to remember. If they do not concur with your own views, please feel free to substitute your own sentiments in place of the one I have expressed. The point is that to remember the words and to deliver the story with sincerity I have a picture in my mind.

An Example:

You will see that I have broken up the piece into the succinct phrases. This is the way I personally deliver them. In the Blue Book I make a forward dash between the words so that I know the delivery I have chosen. You can do the same, or mark the traditional way it is said in your Lodge. e.g., 'The 24-inch Gauge is to measure our work, / the common Gavel to knock off all superfluous knobs and excrescences, / and the Chisel to further smooth...' and so on.

When I come to the end of a passage or to a point where I feel a dramatic pause in the delivery is required, I mark a double forward slash (//) – do not leave the pregnant pauses too long or the IPM will give you a prompt.

The phrase in *italics* is common to the three degrees. There are many sections in the Blue Book that are similar in each degree with only a small phrase or a word change to set them apart. I underline the common phrases in my Blue Book; this makes those parts that are unique look smaller and that gives me a bit of hope that the part to learn is not so big. Having learned the common phrases, reaching them it is like a rest point, it gives me time to think of what comes next.

The phrases, words or letters picked out in **bold** are significant and are either key phrases or part of a memory key.

The Working Tools of an EAFM.

The working tools of an EAFM remind me that life is a balance.

By command of the WM I now present to you the working tools of an Entered Apprentice Freemason:

> They are the 24-inch Gauge, the Common Gavel, and Chisel.
> These tools are in front of you as you stand at the pedestal and make an excellent memory aid. We first describe the actual use of the tools, then the

symbolic. This is the common format through the three degrees.

The 24-inch Gauge is to measure our work, the Common Gavel to knock off all superfluous knobs and excrescences, and the Chisel to further smooth and prepare the stone and render it fit for the hands of the more expert workman.

But, as we are not all operative Masons, but rather free and accepted or speculative, we apply these tools to our morals.

In this sense, the 24-in Gauge represents the twenty-four hours of the day, part to be spent in prayer to Almighty God, (man cannot live by bread alone) part in labour and refreshment, (you must work to earn your bread) and part in serving a friend or Brother in time of need, without detriment to ourselves or connections. (No man is an island; we all need a little help)

The Common Gavel represents the force of conscience, which should keep down all vain and unbecoming thoughts which might obtrude during any of the aforementioned periods, (pride in our endeavours is good it drives us to excel. Conceit on the other hand is not a grace) so that our words and actions may ascend unpolluted to the Throne of Grace.

The Chisel points out to us the advantages of education, by which means alone we are rendered

fit members of regularly organised Society.
(Applied with precision to fashion and refine)

To help remember this piece there is an order you may find of use. The working tools of an EAFM are not too difficult to remember but to illustrate the principle; I will first go through them, after which, you will copy me! The first section is as follows:

They are the 24-inch **G**AUGE, the **C**ommon **G**AVEL, and **C**HISEL.

You will see that I have picked out in bold the first letter at the start of each word of the salient phrase, they are; GC followed by GC so we have GCGC which is pronounced Gee Cee, Gee Cee, which to my twisted mind is made memorable as Juicy, Juicy. The workings of the mind are, fortunately, a personal issue and in the normal course of events you do not have to explain or justify the distorted ramblings that take place in there.

The next passage is: GCGC again

The 24-inch **G**AUGE is to measure our work,
The **C**OMMON **G**AVEL to knock off all superfluous knobs and excrescences,
and the **C**HISEL to further smooth etc.

Then we have one of those common phrases; *But, as we are not all operative Masons etc.*

Then back to GCGC

Masonic Mnemonics

24-in GAUGE represents the twenty-four hours of the day;

The COMMON GAVEL represents the force of conscience;

The CHISEL points out to us the advantages of education;

If you have a problem with a particular line and sometimes it seems that the mind refuses to remember a particular word, try linking it back to a word that comes easily off the tongue in the preceding line.

Take for example: The Common Gavel represents the force of conscience, with conscience being the problem word. Try linking the syllable **COM** in the word common with **CON** in **the word** conscience. Now when you say "The **Com**mon Gavel" the mind has a few moments to make the connection ready for "represents the force of **con**science"

For the next section I use **O**ld **A**ge **P**ensioner to direct my attention to the order of those words which are less commonly used in daily language.

Which should keep down all vain and unbecoming thoughts which might **O**btrude during any of the **A**forementioned **P**eriods,

To recap on the system:
- Break up the work into sections, each section relating to a particular part.
- Look for a pattern; find some relationship that you can link to a mnemonic or phrase that is memorable.
- State the obvious; it gives you confidence that you

know what you are doing and may help when you stand there and are struck dumb.
- Pick out those words that convey the message and link them.
- Mark your Blue Book. You do not need to write much, just the mark will trigger the process.

The Learning Process:
- Think about the context and meaning of the section.
- Learn the first line or key phrase.
- Link the key phrase to the position you or the candidate will be in to deliver the passage.
- Build this up by adding key words, those that convey the essence of the text (marked in **bold**).
- Once you are confident with the above, start work on the detail of the text.

You will find that some sections come to you quickly and easily, others take time and seem to resist absorption. There is no rule, Masonic or otherwise, that says this must be learned in a particular way. Take the path of least resistance; pick up those sections that are easy first. Work on those that are not, one line at a time until you get to a few obstinate words, look back in the text that you are sure of and you will find a word or syllable that you can use as a trigger for the one that you cannot seem to fix.

To Open the Lodge

Having established the basic method, we can now apply it to the Opening of the Lodge. This can be learnt as easily for all three degrees as it can for any individual degree since they are similar. Closing the Lodge in the First can also be learnt with the opening by noting how little they differ.

It is best viewed from the Master's position with the other officers learning the opening in total. Many Lodges go round the junior officers of Lodge asking the questions in turn, others question the two Wardens.

Open (o) and Closing (c)

When opening a Lodge we question all Officers. When closing we question just the two Wardens.

WMo   Brethren. Assist me to **open** the Lodge.
WMc   Brethren. Assist me to **close** the Lodge.
WMo   Bro…Name What is the **first** care of every Mason?

(It is first because it is the first part of the opening)

WMc   Bro **JW**…….What is the **constant** care of every Mason?

(Close = Constant, link the Cs)

WMo   Direct that duty to be done.
WMc   Direct that duty to be done.
WMo   Bro **Name** The next care?
WMc   Bro **JW** The next care?

(Address the name of the Brother before the Lodge is open as those present have not yet been proved Masons; address the position when the Lodge is open)

WMo Bro. SW, the next care?
WMc Bro. SW, the next care?
WMo To order, Brethren, in the First Degree.
WMc To order, Brethren, in the First Degree.
WMo Bro. JW, how many **Principal Officers** are there **in the Lodge**?
WMo Bro. SW, how many **Assistant Officers** are there?

Junior Officers are asked about their Situation and Duty, Senior Officers are asked about their Place, and why they are placed there.

WMo The situation of the **Tyler** or **Outer Guard**?
WMo His duty?
WMo The situation of the **Inner Guard**?
WMo His duty?

Bro. JD,
WMo Your situation?
WMo Your duty?

Bro. SD,
WMo Your situation?
WMo Your duty?

Bro. JW.
WMo Your place in the Lodge?

Masonic Mnemonics

WMo   Why are you placed there?

Bro. SW,

WMo   Your place in the Lodge?
WMc   Your **constant** place in the Lodge?
WMo   Why are you placed there?
WMc   Why are you placed there?
SWc   As the sun sets in the West to close the day, so the Senior Warden is placed in the West; - (This is one of those pieces of ritual that seems to cause problems and best remembered by a phrase given to me by my DC, "It is As the Sun Sets as it is the **Ass** end of the meeting)

IPM

WMo   The Master's place?
WMo   Why is he placed there?
WMo   Then Brethren, the Lodge being duly formed, before I declare it open...Let us;
WMc   Brethren, before we close the Lodge. Let us with all **reverence** and **humility** express our gratitude to the GAU for favours already received, and may he continue to **preserve** our order by **cementing** and **adorning** it with every **moral** and **social** virtue.

The order of the word in the closing prayer causes problems for most; the last two can usually be linked to the label in Brothers' underwear. The three before are in reverse alphabetical order but I have heard it suggested that we should be pickled in concrete and displayed on a wall. Whatever works for you!

The point I am trying to make is this: you can learn the opening and closing by the method of rote (mechanical repetition of something so that it is remembered, often without real understanding of its meaning or significance). However if you look at the phrases used you can see a pattern and by understanding what you are doing, i.e. explaining the position and duty of each office and recognising that there are a few question asked repeatedly to each office in turn, as they are ranked in the Lodge, the task of opening and closing can be simplified. You can also see that we have many phrases which are exactly the same with just a change of a word or two depending on which end of the ceremony you are dealing with. You can mark the common phrases in your Blue Book accordingly.

Once opened in the first the form of the next stage of the meeting follows the acronym **M.O.S.**

Minutes, **O**bituaries, **S**alutes.

The Business of the Evening

I will go through the First Degree in some detail, pointing out those parts I feel significant. The same process can be used for the Second and Third Degrees which I will omit in detail but the later sections show the three degrees together and the small differences between them.

The phrase underlined is the start of each section. It provides the trigger when combined with the visual aid of what is actually happening in the Lodge and is the key phrase for the Lodge Mind Map. The phrases, words or letters picked out in bold are significant and are either key phrases or part of a memory key.

You can hold a virtual ceremony in your mind with a simple plan layout of your Lodge and the first phrase at each position the candidate moves to. The phrases underlined at the start of each new piece are triggered by the candidate as he arrives at a new position. I know of a farmer who has his barn laid out with those huge fertiliser bags in the warden's position. He and his dogs practise parts of the ceremonies, I believe his dogs are quite proficient as Wardens. I myself travel on business and use the time travelling to hold mental ceremonies. I do not recommend you try to do the whole ceremony as interruptions are inevitable and are not going to help your concentration or build your confidence. I suggest you run through the ceremony in sections and using your map, make sure you know the first line and the position in which it is spoken. Also, most importantly, why!

Context:

A man is about to be made a mason; we must first check his eligibility.

He is a free man, unbound by any duty to another master.

Mature years; to make a commitment he must be old enough to know his own mind.

That he can say with honesty that he has a belief in something bigger than himself. The Great Architect of the universe, be it a he, she or it.

Open Lodge; all can see this man, he cannot see them.

The first part for both the JD and WM follows the order of events in becoming a Mason. A friend will ask if you wish to consider Freemasonry; you will be questioned about your belief in a supreme being. You will be proposed in open Lodge, people will speak well of you and your application to become a Mason will be put to the vote.

The First Degree

IG   WM, at the door ………privileges of Ancient Freemasonry.

WM   *How does he hope to obtain those privileges?* (The same for each degree)

IG   By the help of **God, being free and of good report**. (The three requirements to become a Mason)

WM   *The tongue of good report* has already been heard in his favour; (Proposed in open Lodge) do you Bro IG vouch that he is **properly prepared**.

IG   I do WM.

WM   *Then let him be admitted in due form. Bro Deacons.* (The same for each degree)

Masonic Mnemonics

The Candidate viewed as a Horse Shoe!

       Hoodwink
       Cable Tow
                           Left Breast
Right Arm
                           Left Knee
Right Heel
                           Left Shoe

When you look at the candidate there is regularity about him. In the first degree we step off with the Left foot, look to the left foot and see the **Left Shoe**. Lift your eyes up, over and down. It should look like a horse shoe.

Second degree looks the same but starting with the **Right Shoe and no Cable Tow**.

We march Left, Right; first, second. Arm and Heel non-shoe side in both degrees.

You kneel on your left bare knee to take your obligation in the First Degree and on your right bare knee for the Second Degree. I remember this as I was told it was so we could take our obligation with our bare flesh touching Mother Earth, I know there is bound to be another view.

WM   [Gavels *] Mr surname, as no person can be made a Mason unless he is **free** and of **mature age**, **I demand of you**, are you a free man and of the full age of twenty-one years? (Call his name; get his attention before you speak again)

Cand I am.

Masonic Mnemonics

WM — <u>Thus assured, I will thank you to kneel,</u> while the **Blessing of Heaven** is invoked on our proceedings. (As the candidate kneels you stand, [Gavel] a basic rule; when the candidate is up the Master is down and when the Master is down the candidate should be up.)

WM — <u>Mr surname in all cases of difficulty and danger</u> in whom do you put your trust?

Cand — In God.

WM — <u>Right glad am I to find your faith so well founded</u>; for relying on such **sure support**, you may safely **arise and follow your leader** with a firm but humble confidence, for where the **name of God is invoked we trust no danger** can ensue. [pause] Let the Cand rise (Sit; do not let them get away! Gavel!) (So far we have confirmed the questions asked of every candidate)

WM — [Gavels *] <u>The Brethren from the North, East, South and West</u> will take notice that Mr surname is about to **pass in view before them**, to show that he is the Candidate, properly prepared, and a fit and proper person to be made a Mason.

(Once round the Lodge, **PPPP**, **P**ast the Master, the only time this happens, JD – Bro JW I **p**resent to you, JD – Bro SW, I **p**resent to you, SW – WM I **p**resent to you. Past and 3 presents)

Masonic Mnemonics 21

We must now check that he joins us for noble reasons, not to gain some pecuniary advantage from membership.

SW   WM, I present to you Mr B a Candidate **properly prepared** to be made a Mason.

WM   <u>Bro. SW, your presentation shall be attended to</u>, for which purpose I will address a **few questions** to the Candidate, which I trust he will **answer with candour**.

WM   <u>Mr surname; do you seriously declare on your honour</u> that, unbiased by the **improper solicitation of friends** against your own inclination, and **uninfluenced by mercenary** or other **unworthy motives**, (**umum** remembered as umm, a question?) you freely and voluntarily offer yourself a Candidate for the mysteries and privileges of Ancient Freemasonry? (The S in seriously reminds me in this question the key phrase is Solicitation)

Cand   I do.

WM   <u>Do you likewise pledge yourself</u> that you are **prompted** to solicit those **privileges** from a **favourable opinion preconceived** of the Institution, a general **desire for knowledge**, and a sincere wish to render yourself more **extensively serviceable** to your fellow creatures? (The P in pledge is the key for, Prompted, privileges and preconceived)

Cand   I do.

WM   <u>Do you **further** seriously declare on your honour,</u> that, **avoiding fear** on the one hand, and rashness on the other, you will **steadily persevere** through the ceremony of your Initiation, and, **if admitted**, will afterwards act and abide by the **ancient usages** and **established customs** of the Order? (The F in further is my key for fear and persevere, the two words rhyme!)

Cand   I will.

The three pledges run;

    Seriously declare on your honour

    Likewise pledge yourself

    Further seriously declare on your honour

WM   <u>Bro SW, You will direct the JD</u> to instruct the Candidate to advance to the Pedestal in due form.

SW   Bro JD, It is the WM's command that you instruct the Candidate to advance to the Pedestal in due form.

The man will now be made a Mason and he needs to know what is expected of him.

WM   <u>Mr. surname it is my duty to inform you that Masonry is free</u>, and requires a perfect **freedom of inclination** in every Candidate for its Mysteries; it is founded on the **purest principles of piety**

Masonic Mnemonics 23

  and virtue; it possesses many great and invaluable privileges; and in **order to secure** those privileges to **worthy** men, and **we trust to worthy men alone**, vows of fidelity are required; but let me assure you, that in those vows there is **nothing incompatible** with your **civil, moral, or religious duties**; are you therefore willing to take a solemn obligation, founded on the Principles I have stated, to keep inviolate the **Secrets and Mysteries** of the Order? (This never seems a problem, only the order of civil, moral, or religious duties and they run alphabetically)

Cand I am.

WM <u>Then you will kneel on you **left** knee, turn your **right** foot out</u> to form a square, give me your **right hand** which I place on this book, which is the Volume of the Sacred Law, while your **left** will be employed in supporting a pair of compasses, one point extended to your naked ....
<u>Repeat your names at length and say after me</u>......

The obligation; this is marked in the form that I ask the candidate to repeat after me and divided into what I consider the memorable sections and how I remember the section. The first section is very similar in each degree.

Name
<u>WM Rises and gavels</u> *I* ....*in the presence of/ the* **Great Architect of the Universe**,/ *and of this worthy, worshipful,*

and warranted/ *Lodge of* **Free and Accepted Masons** /, *regularly assembled/ and properly dedicated, /of my own free will and accord,/ do hereby,/ and hereon,/* **sincerely and solemnly**/ *promise and swear,/ that I will always hele,/ conceal,/ and never reveal*// (in each degree this changes slightly and is easy to get wrong)

The secret!

any part or parts,/ point or points/ of the secrets/ or mysteries/ of or belonging to/ (**F**) Free and Accepted Masons/ in Masonry/ which may heretofore/ have been known by me,/ or shall now/ or at any future period/ be communicated to me,/ unless it be/ to a true and lawful/ Brother or Brothers,/ and not even/ to him or them,/ until after due trial,/ strict examination,/ or sure information/ from a well-known Brother/ that he or they/ are worthy/ of that confidence;/ or in the body/ of a just,/ perfect/ and regular Lodge/ of (**A**) Ancient Freemasons.//

The small print

I further solemnly **promise**/ that I will not write those secrets,/ indite,/ carve,/ mark,/ engrave,/ or otherwise them delineate,/ (IC-MED ick-med) or cause or suffer/ it to be so done by others,/ if in my power/ to prevent it,/ on anything, movable/ or immovable/ under the canopy of Heaven,/ whereby/ or whereon/ any letter,/ character,/ or figure,/ or the least trace/ of a letter,/ character,/ or figure,/ may become legible,/ or intelligible/ to myself/ or anyone in the world,/ so that our secret arts/ and hidden mysteries/ may improperly/ become known/ through my unworthiness.//

The Pledge

These **several** *points/ I solemnly swear to observe,/ without evasion,/ equivocation,/ or mental reservation/ of any kind,/* in the certain knowledge/ that on the violation/ of any of them/ I shall be branded/ as a wilfully/ perjured individual,/ void of all moral worth,/ and totally unfit/ to be received/ into this worshipful Lodge,/ or any other/ warranted Lodge,/ or society of men/ who prize honour/ and virtue/ above the external advantages/ of rank and fortune.//

So help me God, */ and keep me steadfast/ in this/ my* **Great and** *Solemn/ Obligation/*of an Entered Apprentice Freemason//

Lodge of Free and Accepted Masons (This phrase comes up three times in a slightly different form. Visualise an **Al-f-a** Romeo Car. The order runs thus:

Al = All = Lodge of Free, and Accepted Masons;
F = Free and Accepted Masons in Masonry,
A = Ancient Freemasons)
I further solemnly **promise**; – in the first and second degrees you 'promise', in the third it's 'engage myself'

These **several** *points*; – in the first and second degree, in the third it is 'All these points'

Great and *Solemn/ Obligation*; – Only the first degree has a 'Great' and solemn obligation, the other two are simply Solemn Obligations.

First Degree Masters map up to the end of the obligation

SW

      SW   WM I present to you

8/ Bro. SW, your presentation shall be attended to
9/ Mr surname do you seriously declare on your honour
10/ Do you likewise pledge yourself
11/ Do you further seriously declare on your honour
12/ Bro SW, You will direct the JD

IG at the Door

1/ How does he hope to obtain those privileges?
2/ The tongue of good report
3/ Then let him be admitted in due form

At the Kneeling Stool

4/ Mr surname, as no person can be made a Mason
5/ Mr surname in all cases of difficulty and danger
6/ Right glad am I to find your faith so well founded;
7/ The Brethren from the North, East, South and West

JW

13/ Mr. surname it is my duty to inform you
14/ Then you will kneel on your left knee turn your right foot out
15/ Repeat your several names at length and say after me…
16/ WM Rises and gavels I…………..
17/ Obligation

WM

To demonstrate the principle I have split the map in two. In practice I would make this four; you should divide this up into sections that inform and do not confuse. As they are written now, for demonstration purposes, I would find them too 'busy' to be helpful.

WM   pauses to remove the compasses

WM   <u>What you have repeated may be considered but as a</u> **serious promise**; as a pledge of your Fidelity, and to render it a **Solemn Obligation**, you will seal it with your **lips on the V.S.L.** which lies before you.

(Wands come down and All drop the Sign of F......y. This can be a sticking point, he is kneeling there and you have finished. Once the VSL has been saluted he has made his obligation and may now be part of the fraternity, thus he is entitled to light)

WM   <u>Having been kept a considerable time in a state of darkness</u>, what in your **present situation** is the **predominant wish** of your heart?

Cand   Light.

WM   <u>Bro JD, in due time let that blessing be restored</u>. [WM raises Gavel high and "marks" in the air Gavels All Clap simultaneously with the sound of the Gavel].

WM	<u>Having been restored to the blessing of material light</u>, let me direct your attention to what we consider the **three** Great, though **emblematical**, Lights in Freemasonry: They are the **V.S.L, the Square and Compasses**: the Sacred Writings are to rule and govern our Faith, the Square to regulate our actions, and the Compasses to keep us in due bounds with all mankind, particularly our Brethren in Freemasonry. (I remember 'particularly our Brethren in Freemasonry'; it is a unique phrase and is the end of the obligation)
WM	***<u>Rise, duly obligated</u> "Brother" among Masons***. [WM sits].
WM	<u>You are now enabled to discover the</u> **three Lesser** Lights in Freemasonry; they are situated **East, South & West**, and are meant to represent the Sun, Moon, and Master of the Lodge: the Sun to rule the day, the Moon to govern the night, and the Master to rule and direct his Lodge. (The first time the lesser lights are spoken of they start at the East then South and West. Second time they are mentioned it starts in the South then West and finishes in with East. Thus; East, South, West, East. This is one of those points where it dries up; move them towards you, one step short of the stool. The next section seems to flow and is not difficult to remember as it has been a big part of moving

Masonic Mnemonics

through the deacon's office)

WM **"Brother"** surname <u>by your meek and candid behaviour</u> this evening you have symbolically escaped two great dangers, but there was a third which, traditionally, would have awaited you until the **latest period of your existence**. The dangers you have escaped are those of **stabbing or strangling**, [poignard; WM "on his Cuff"] for on your entrance into the Lodge the point of this **sharp sword** was **presented to your naked left breast**, to imply that, had you rashly attempted to rush forward you would have been an accessory to your own death by stabbing, not so the Brother who held it for he would have remained firm and done his duty [WM returns poignard]

There was likewise this cable-tow, [WM slips it over his wrist and pulls it tight] with a running noose about your neck, which would have rendered any attempt at retreat equally fatal. [WM gives Cable Tow to IPM]

(The entrance of the candidate was at one time, and in some lodges it still is, a candidate moving round the Lodge with a drawn sword held to his chest by one brother and the cable-tow held by another brother following on behind. The candidate was indeed in danger if he moved forwards or backwards.)

But the danger which, traditionally would have awaited you until your **latest hour** was the **"Physical Penalty"** at one time associated with the obligation of an E.A. F.M. that you would rather have had [WM stands and does the Sign to illustrate] your ...., than improperly disclose the Secrets entrusted to you. [WM sits].

WM   The inclusion of such a penalty is unnecessary, for the obligation you have taken this evening is binding upon you so long as you shall live.

The means of identification, the word and the sign.

<u>Having entered on the great and solemn Obligation</u> of an E.A.F.M, I am now permitted to inform you that there are several Degrees in Freemasonry, with peculiar secrets restricted to each; these, however, are not **communicated** indiscriminately, but are **conferred** on Candidates according to **merit and abilities**. I shall therefore proceed to entrust you with the Secrets of this Degree, or those Marks by which we are known to each other, and distinguished from the rest of the World; but must premise for your general information that all Squares, Levels and Perpendiculars, are true and proper Signs to know a Mason by; you are therefore expected to **stand perfectly erect,** your feet formed in a square, **your body** being thus considered an **emblem of your mind**, and **your feet** of the **rectitude of your actions**.

WM   <u>You will now take a short pace towards me</u> with your left foot, bringing the right heel into its hollow; "that" is the first regular step in Free-

Masonic Mnemonics

masonry, and it is in this position the Secrets of the Degree are communicated; they consist of a Sign, Grip or Token, and Word. [WM stand]

<u>Place you hand in this position</u>, ...of a ...... The Sign is given by placing.....to.............. ....

This, as you will perceive, alludes to the Symbolic Penalty of this Degree which implied that, as a man of honour, an E.A.F.M. would rather have had, **please copy me**, his .... than improperly disclose the Secrets entrusted to him.

<u>The Grip or Token</u> is given by a distinct pressure of the ..... on the ....

This, when properly given and received serves to distinguish a Brother by night as well as by day; this Grip demands a Word, a Word highly prized amongst Masons, as the guard to their privileges, too much caution cannot, therefore, be observed in communicating it; it should never be given at length, but always by letter or syllable; to enable you to do this I must tell you what that word is: it is ....; please spell it after me... As during the course of the Ceremony you will be called on for this Word, the JD will now dictate the answers you are to give.

WM   What is this?

WM   What does this Grip demand?

WM   Give me that Word.

WM	Letter it and I will begin… ….
WM	This word is derived from the…….which stood at the porch way or entrance to King Solomon's Temple, so named after…., the great……………., a Prince and Ruler in Israel; the import of the Word is "in ….." Pass …
SW	WM, I present to you, Bro. Surname.
WM	<u>Bro. SW, I delegate you</u> the important duty of investing our newly made Brother with the distinguishing badge of an E.A.F.M.
SW	Bro. B, surname by the WM's command, I invest you ….. never disgrace "that" badge, that badge will never disgrace you.

These are the rules of behaviour and the virtues we aspire to.

| WM | <u>Let me add to the observations</u> of the SW, that you are never to put on that badge, should you be about to visit a Lodge wherein there is a Brother with whom you are at **variance**, or against whom you **entertain animosity**; in such a case, it is expected you will **invite him to withdraw**, in order amicably to **settle your differences**, which if happily effected, you may then **clothe, enter the Lodge**, and work with that **love and harmony** which should at all times **characterise** Freemasons. But if, unfortunately, your differences |

are of such a nature as not to be so **easily adjusted**, it were better that one or both of you **retire**, than that the **harmony** of the Lodge should be **disturbed by your presence**.

WM   <u>Bro JD, you will place</u> our Bro. at the N.E. part of the Lodge.

WM   <u>Bro A. at the erection of all stately and superb edifices</u> it is customary to lay the **first or foundation stone** at the N.E. corner of the building; you, being newly initiated into Freemasonry, are placed at the N.E. part of the Lodge, figuratively to **represent that stone**; and from the foundation laid this evening may you raise a superstructure perfect in its parts and honourable to the builder.

You now stand to all external appearance a just and upright E.A.F.M, and I give it you in strong terms of recommendation ever to continue and act as such; indeed, I shall immediately proceed to put your principles in some measure to the test, by calling on you to exercise that virtue, which may justly be **denominated the distinguishing characteristic (DDC)**, (like BBC, only not) of a Freemason's heart - I mean Charity. I need not here dilate upon its excellencies; no doubt it has often been felt and practised by you; suffice it to say, that it has the approbation of heaven and earth, and, like its sister Mercy, blesses him who gives as well as him who receives.

In a society so widely extended as Freemasonry, the branches of which are spread over the four quarters of the globe, it cannot be denied that we have many members of **rank and opulence**, neither can it be concealed that among the thousands who range under its banners, there are some who, perhaps from circumstances of **unavoidable calamity and misfortune**, are reduced to the lowest ebb of poverty and distress.

On their behalf it is our usual custom to awaken the feelings of every newly made Brother, by making such a claim on his charity as his **circumstances in life may fairly warrant**; whatever therefore you feel disposed to give, you will deposit with the JD; it will be thankfully received and faithfully applied.

JD   Have you anything to give in the cause of charity?

WM   <u>I congratulate you, my Brother</u>, on the **honourable sentiments** by which you are actuated, likewise on the inability which in the present instance precludes (PIP) you from gratifying them; believe me, this trial was not made with a view to sport with your feelings; far from us be any such intention; it was done for three especial reasons,

first, as I have already premised, to put your principles in some measure to the test;

secondly, **to evince to the Brethren** that you had neither **money nor metallic substance** about you, for if you had, the ceremony of your **Initiation thus far must have been repeated**;

Masonic Mnemonics 35

and, lastly, as a **warning to your heart**, that should you at any future period meet a **friend or Brother in distressed circumstances** who might **solicit your assistance**, you will remember the **peculiar moment** in which you were admitted into Freemasonry, **poor, penniless and half clad** and cheerfully embrace the opportunity of practising **that virtue you now profess to admire**.

WM <u>As in the course of the evening</u> you have been called on for certain fees for your Initiation, it is only right you should know by what Authority we act. This is our **Charter or Warrant** [WM indicates, JD points with his Wand base] from the **Grand Lodge of England**, which is open for your **inspection** on this, or any **future Lodge evening**;

this is our **book of Constitutions**, and these are **our By-laws**, both of which I recommend to your serious perusal, as by the former you will be taught the **important duties you owe to the Craft in general**, and by the latter, those you owe to **this Lodge, name, in particular**.

WM <u>You are now at liberty to retire,</u> in order to restore yourself to your personal comforts, and on your return to the Lodge I shall direct your attention to a **Charge** to be given by the SW, **founded on the excellence of our Institution and the qualifications of its members**. And may I be the first to congratulate you on taking your first **regular step in Freemasonry**.

IG	Bro JW the ADC and the Candidate on their return, seek admission.
WM	[Gavels] Brethren, I claim your attention while the SW delivers the Charge.

Charge. DC To Order Brethren [DC gives a "clap"].

WM	This concludes the Ceremony of Initiation. The WM will now address the Secretary and enquire "the remainder of the business of the evening".

First Degree Masters map after the obligation.

SW

SW   WM I present to you
29/ Bro. SW, I delegate you
30/ Let me add to the observations
31/ Bro JD, you will place

IG at the Door

JW

NE part of the Lodge
32/ Bro A. at the erection of all stately and superb edifices
33/ I congratulate you, my Brother,
18/ What you have repeated may be considered
19/ Having been kept a considerable time in a state of darkness,
20/ Having been restored to the blessing of material light
21/ Bro JD, in due time let that blessing be restored
22/ **Rise, duly obligated**

23/ You are now enabled to discover
24/ "Brother" surname by your meek and candid behaviour
25/ Having entered on the great and solemn Obligation
26/ You will now take a short pace towards me
27/ Place you hand in this position
28/ The Grip or Token
34/ As in the course of the evening
35/ You are now at liberty to retire,
36/ [Gavels] Brethren, I claim your attention
37/ This concludes the Ceremony of Initiation

WM

If when the candidate is moving about the Lodge you can work through the framework and morality of the degree, the **Context**, and know the opening phrase when the candidate reaches each position in the ceremony, the **Content**, you can consider yourself comfortable with the First Degree. Once you have confidence in your understanding of the ceremony, you can now devote your time to the **Detail** of the individual sections. You may be pleasantly surprised with how you cope with remembering these sections. If you know the story you are trying to convey and you know the path through the ceremony the candidate is to follow. There is only one thing left that requires your attention. The words!

Second and third degrees

The Second and Third Degree can be viewed as two parts – one being those sections that are common with a word or two changed as appropriate, and those sections that are unique to the degree.

The questions are put in the degree that the candidate has attained with the exclusions of the inferior degrees. The following comes immediately after the business of the evening has been announced.

WM: I must now ask all those below the rank of a **Fellowcraft/Master Mason**, *with the exception of Bro surname to retire from the Temple for a short time.*

WM: Brethren, Brother surname is this evening a Candidate to be **Passed/Raised** *to the* **Second/Third** Degree, *but it is first requisite that he give proofs of proficiency in the* **Former/Second**. *I shall therefore proceed to put the necessary questions.*

Questions before passing

These questions follow the progression of all candidates into Freemasonry.

WM-second   Bro A. B. where were you first prepared to be made a Mason?

Cand   In my heart.

WM-second   Where next?

Cand	In a convenient room adjoining the Lodge.
WM-second	Describe the mode of your preparation. (*Left shoe Horse shoe*)
Cand	I was divested of all money & metallic substances and hoodwinked, my right arm, left breast & knee were made bare, my right heel was slipshod and a cable-tow placed about my neck.
WM-second	Where were you made a Mason?
Cand	In the body of a Lodge, Just, Perfect and Regular.
WM-second	And when?
Cand	When the sun was at its meridian.
WM-second	In this country Freemasons' lodges are usually held in the evening; how do you account for that which at first view appears a paradox?
Cand	The earth constantly revolving on its axis in its orbit round the Sun and Freemasonry being universally spread over its surface, it necessarily follows that the Sun must always be at its meridian with respect to Freemasonry.
WM-second	What is Freemasonry?
Cand	A peculiar system of morality, veiled in

	allegory and illustrated by Symbols.
WM-second	Name the Grand Principals on which the order is founded.
Cand	Brotherly Love, Relief and Truth.
WM-second	Who are fit and proper persons to be made Masons?
Cand	Just, upright and free men of mature age, sound judgement and strict morals.
WM-second	How do you know yourself to be a Mason?
Cand	By the regularity of my Initiation, repeated trials and approbation, and a willingness at all times to undergo an examination when properly called on.
WM-second	How do you demonstrate the proof of being a Mason to others?
Cand	By signs, tokens & the Perfect Points of my Entrance.
WM:	These, Brethren, are the usual Questions. If any Brother desires me to put others, I will do so.

Questions before rising

WM-third	How were you prepared to be passed to the Second Degree? (*Right shoe Horse shoe*)

Cand	In a manner somewhat similar to the former, save that in this Degree I was not hoodwinked, my left arm, breast and knee were made bare and my left heel was slipshod.
WM-third	On what were you admitted?
Cand	The square.
WM-third	What is a square?
Cand	An angle of 90 degrees or the or the fourth part of a circle.
WM-third	What are the peculiar objects of research in this Degree?
Cand	The hidden mysteries of Nature and Science.
WM-third	As it is the hope of reward that sweetens labour, where did our ancient brethren go to receive their wages?
Cand	Into the middle chamber of King Solomon's Temple.
WM-third	How did they receive them?
Cand	Without scruple or diffidence.
WM-third	Why in this peculiar manner?
Cand	Without scruple, well knowing they were justly entitled to them, and without diffidence, from the great reliance they

placed on the integrity of their employers in those days.

WM-third   What were the names of the two great Pillars which were placed at the porchway or entrance of King Solomon's Temple?

Cand   That on the left was called ——, and that on the right ——.

WM-third   What are their separate and conjoint significations?

Cand   The former denotes in strength, the latter, to establish; and when conjoined, stability, for God said, 'In strength I will establish this Mine house to stand firm for ever.'

WM: *These are the usual questions; I will put others if any Brother wishes me to do so.*

After the questions the next section is the giving of a password and pass-grip, there is little difference between the degrees.

WM Bro surname do you pledge your honour as a man and your fidelity as a **Mason/Craftsman**, *that you will steadily persevere through the Ceremony of your being* **Passed to the Degree of a Fellowcraft/Raised to the sublime Degree of a Master Mason**?

Cand   I do.

WM   *Do you likewise pledge yourself that you will*

Masonic Mnemonics

> *conceal what I shall now impart to you with the same strict caution as the other secrets in Masonry?*

Cand   I do.

WM   *Then I will entrust you with a test of merit, which is a Pass-grip and Pass-word, leading to the Degree to which you seek to be admitted. (Stands and takes the candidate's right hand in his own right hand and holds it)*

The Pass-grip is given by a distinct p s e of the ......between the ...etc. This Pass-grip demands a Word, which is S......h/T....C

The WM then explains the password and its import. You must be particularly careful to remember this word, as without it you cannot gain admission into a Lodge in a superior degree.

WM   *Pass S.../T..C..*

After this the candidate retires from the Lodge which is then opened in the superior degree.

Second and Third Degree openings have much in common and can be marked up as such.

WM   *Brethren, assist me to open the Lodge in the* **Second/Third** *Degree.*

WM   *Brother Junior Warden, what is the first care of every –* Craftsman/Master Mason.

JW	*To see that the Lodge is properly tyled.*
WM	*Direct that duty to be done.*
JW	*Brother Inner Guard, see that the Lodge is properly tyled.*
IG	*Brother Junior Warden, the Lodge is properly tyled.*

JW knocks, Sign, to WM: The Lodge is properly tyled.

WM	*Brother Senior Warden, the next care?*
SW	*To see that the Brethren appear to order as –* **Craftsmen/Master Mason**.
WM	*To order Brethren in the –* **Second/Third** *Degree.*
WM	*Brother Junior Warden, are you a –* **Fellow Craft Freemason/Master Mason**.
JW	*I am, Worshipful Master, try me and prove me.*
WM	*By what* **instrument/instruments** *in architecture will you be proved?*
JW	*The Square.*

The Square and Compass

WM	*What is a Square?*
JW	*An angle of 90 Degrees, or the fourth part of a Circle.*

In the third degree no answer is given.

WM	*Being yourself acquainted with the proper method, you will prove the Brethren* **Craftsmen/Master Masons** *by signs and demonstrate that proof to me by copying their example.*
JW	*Brethren, it is the Worshipful Master's command that you prove yourselves –* **Craftsmen/Master Masons** *by signs.*
JW	*Worshipful Master, the Brethren have proved themselves –* **Craftsmen/Master Masons** *and in obedience to your command I thus copy their example.*
WM:	*Brother Junior Warden, I acknowledge the correctness of the Sign.*

You then have the exchanges between the Master and Wardens for the third degree.

WM-third	Brother Junior Warden, Whence come you?
JW:	The East. (He is in the South, heading West to the SW position)
WM-third	Brother Senior Warden, whither directing your course?
SW	The West. (He is in the West, heading East to the Masters Chair)

WM-third	**What** inducement have you to leave the East and go to the West?
JW:	To seek for that which was lost, which, by your instruction and our own industry, we hope to find.
WM-third	**What** is that which was lost?
SW	The genuine secrets of a Master Mason.
WM-third	**How** came they lost?
JW	By the untimely death of our Master, Hiram Abiff.
WM-third	**Where** do you hope to find them?
SW	With the Centre.
WM-third	**What** is a Centre?
JW	A point within a circle, from which every part of the circumference is equidistant.
WM-third	**Why** with the Centre?
SW	That being a point from which a Master Mason cannot err.
WM-third	We will assist you to repair that loss and may Heaven aid our united endeavours. ——— So mote it be.
WM-third	Brethren, in the name of the Most High, I

> declare the Lodge ……….

Remember this and it will give the prompt for the order of what questions to ask.

What, What, How. ————Where, What, Why.

The directions of the Wardens are memorable because they are the opposite!

The Similarities and the Differences of the Three Degrees.

The first degree is where I started as much has been learned in the Deacon and Warden positions. When I see the three together, I can see that much is the same. I have made keys to help me remember what is different.

The three degrees are laid out in ascending order to enable you to see how much they are alike and the small differences to be remembered.

The lodge being duly formed

WM-first Then Brethren, the Lodge being duly formed, before I declare it open, Let us invoke the assistance of the Great Architect of the Universe on all our undertakings; may our **labours**, thus begun in **order**, be conducted in **peace**, and closed in **harmony**. (**Lop-h** like Joppa or another commonly used key is **Oph**elia)

WM-second Before we open the Lodge in the Second Degree, let us **supplicate** the Grand Geometrician of the Universe, that the **rays**

	of Heaven may **shed their influence** to enlighten us in the **paths of virtue and science**. (Unive**r**se is the word that links **Vir**tue and Science. The syllables ver and vir have the same phonetic sound)
WM-third	We will assist you to **repair that loss** and may **Heaven aid** our united endeavours.

Declare the lodge open

WM-first	*Brethren, in the name of the* Great Architect of the Universe *I declare the Lodge duly opened* <u>for the purposes of Freemasonry in the **First Degree**</u>.
WM-second	*Brethren, in the name of the* Grand Geometrician of the Universe, *I declare the Lodge duly opened*, on the **Square** for the instruction and improvement of Craftsmen.
WM-third	*Brethren, in the name of the* Most High, *I declare the Lodge duly opened*, on the **Centre** <u>for the purposes of Freemasonry in the **Third Degree**.</u>

(Do not forget once the tools are out and the tracing board is in its right place **AG to the MH**, then you can all sit down)

The opening of the Lodge in the three degrees is always opened in the name relevant to the degree, in the second and third degrees on the square and centre which are both significant to their respective degree. The first and third are the same apart from the word first and third and the second is for the *instruction and improvement of Craftsmen*, which I recall by the phrase 'aye aye Captain'

Knocks

I remember the knocks for each degree thus;

First Degree = ***

From the first to the second it is one (*) for the first degree which you are leaving and (**) for the second degree you are opening in.

From the second to the third it is (**) for the second degree you are in and (*) for the third degree you are opening in.

Hence *** —— * ** —— ** * or 3, 1/2, 2/1, commonly referred to as one and two pence and two and a penny.

At the door of the Lodge

WM   *How does he hope to obtain those privileges?* (The same for each degree)

WM-first The tongue of good report has already been heard in his favour; *do you, Bro. IG, vouch that he is properly prepared?*

WM-second We acknowledge the **propriety of the aid** by which he seeks admission; *do you, Bro. IG, vouch that he is properly prepared* and in

Masonic Mnemonics 51

possession of the Pass grip and Password?

Key = pro-pie-e-**TEE** = **Tea for Two**, it is a song Two = second degree.

WM-third We acknowledge the **powerful aid** by which he seeks admission, *do you, Bro. IG, vouch that he is properly prepared* and in possession of the Pass Grip and Password?

Key = Power-Full = F = Free = three = third degree.

WM *Then let him be admitted in due form. Bro Deacons.* (The same for each degree)

The Kneeling Stool

WM-first Thus assured, I will thank you to *kneel, while the Blessing of Heaven is invoked on* **our proceedings**.

WM-second & third
 Let the Candidate *kneel, while the Blessing of Heaven is invoked on* **what we are about to do**.

The Perambulations

The perambulations in the three degrees run thus;

First degree = Once round the Lodge – **PPPP**: **Past** the Master, the only time this happens, Bro JW I **P**resent to you, Bro SW, I **P**resent to you, SW; WM I **P**resent to you.

Second degree = Twice round the Lodge: SAS and SSAPP (SAP)

First time = **SAS**: **S**alute the WM, **A**dvance to the JW, **S**alute the SW

Knock! (WM Gavels after the candidate has proved the degree he has achieved and calls the Lodge to recognise the candidate)

Second time = **SSAPP**; Salute the WM, Salute the JW, Advance to the SW- **P**ass Grip and **P**assword.

Third degree = Three times round the Lodge: SAS, SSA and SSAPP (SAP).

First time = **SAS**: **S**alute the WM, **A**dvance to the JW, Salute the SW

Second time = **SSA**: Salute the WM, Salute the JW, **A**dvance to the SW

Knock! (WM Gavels after the candidate has proved the degree he has achieved and calls the Lodge to recognise the candidate)

Third time = **SSAPP**: Salute the WM, Salute the JW, Advance to the SW- **P**ass Grip and **P**assword.

Proved in each degree the candidate has attained and in the candidate's attained degree tested for the pass grip and password.

The Brethren Will Take Notice

WM-first *The Brethren* **from the North, East, South and West** *will take notice that* Mr Surname *is about to pass in view before them, to show that he is the Candidate, properly prepared* and a fit and proper person to be made a Mason.

WM-second *The Brethren will take notice that* Bro Surname, who has been regularly initiated into Freemasonry *is about to pass in view before them, to show that he is the Candidate, properly prepared* to be **passed to the Second Degree**.

WM-third T*he Brethren will take notice that* Bro Surname, who has been regularly initiated into Freemasonry, and Passed to the Degree of a Fellowcraft, *is about to Pass in view before them to show that he is the Candidate, properly prepared* to be **Raised to the Third Degree**.

Advance to the Pedestal

WM-first *Bro SW, You will direct the* **JD** *to instruct the Candidate to advance to the* **Pedestal in due form**.

WM-second *Bro SW, you will direct the* **SD** *to instruct the Candidate to advance to the* **East in due form**.

54 — Masonic Mnemonics

WM-third   *Bro SW, you will direct the **SD** to instruct the Candidate to advance to the **East by the proper steps**.*

Key = *Pedestal – <u>due form</u> ……….. east – <u>due form</u> ……….. east – proper steps*

Preparation for the Obligation

WM-second   Bro. surname as in every case the **D**ifferent **D**egrees in Freemasonry are to be kept separate and distinct, **another Obligation** will now be required of you, in many respects similar to that in the former; are you willing to take it? (**DDt**; different degrees… distinct)

WM-third   It is but fair to inform you that **a most serious trial** of your fortitude and fidelity and a **more solemn Obligation** await you. Are you prepared to meet them as you ought? (Mo-s-t; most serious trial… more solemn…)

The Kneeling Stool at the Master's Pedestal

In the first degree we start off with our left foot, so we kneel on our left knee turn the other foot out to form a sq and the right hand is always on the V.S.L. and the left hand is doing something. The second degree changes the knee and foot over and the third degree is both knees and both hands. So

Masonic Mnemonics 55

it runs for knees; Left, Right, Both and for the left hand; compass, square, V.S.L.

WM-first   *Then you will kneel* **on your left knee**; turn your **right** *foot* out to form a square, give me your right hand which I place on this book, which is the Volume of the Sacred Law, while your left.... will be employed in supporting a pair of compasses, one point extended to your naked ......;

Repeat your names at length and say after me.

WM-second   *Then you will kneel* **on your right knee**; *your* **left** *foot formed in a square* place your right hand on the V.S.L., while your left arm will be supported in the angle of the ....;

Repeat your names at length and say after me.

WM-third   *Then you will kneel* **on both knees**, place both hands on the V.S.L.

Repeat your names at length, and say after me.

Obligation

WM-first   I Wonderful Willy Wonker. RAPD *in the presence of the* **Great Architect of the Universe, and of this worthy, worshipful**, and **warranted** *Lodge of* **Free, and Accepted Masons**, *regularly assembled and properly dedicated, of my own free will and accord, do hereby and hereon* **sincerely and**

56 — *Masonic Mnemonics*

solemnly promise and swear, (Wonderful Willy Wonker. RAPD; *Worthy, Worshipful,* **and Warranted**; **R**egularly **A**ssembled and **P**roperly **D**edicated)

WM-second I Wonderful Willy Held. *in the presence of the* **Grand Geometrician of the Universe** *and of this worthy and worshipful Lodge of* **Fellowcraft Freemasons**, *regularly **held**, assembled, and properly dedicated, of my own free will and accord, do hereby and hereon **solemnly** promise and swear,*

(I Wonderful Willy Held corresponds to; *Worthy and Worshipful*; *Regularly* **Held** *Assembled and Properly Dedicated*)

WM-third I Wonderful Willy DC *in the presence of the* **Most High**, *and of this Worthy and Worshipful Lodge of* **Master Masons**, **duly constituted**, *regularly assembled, and properly dedicated, of my own free will and accord, do hereby & hereon* **most solemnly and sincerely** *promise and swear,*

(I Wonderful Willy DC; *Worthy and Worshipful*; **Duly constituted** *Regularly Assembled and Properly Dedicated*)

Divine being (GAU, GGU & MH)

The promise runs to this pattern

sincerely and solemnly—————— **solemnly**————

— most solemnly and sincerely

Wonderful Willy = Two W's *Worthy and Worshipful* Then always Rapd = ***R****egularly **A**ssembled and **P**roperly **D**edicated* (this phrase is always used with the addition of one extra word in the second and two extra words in the third. So it is plus one word each time you go up one degree and for the second degree it is the second word in the phrase. *Regularly **Held** Assembled* etc. For the third degree it is the first two words in the phrase **Duly Constituted**, Regularly Assembled etc)

The three degrees run; Wonker, held, DC.

I further solemnly '**promise**'; – in the first and second degrees you 'promise' in the third it's '**engage myself**'

'***These** several*' points; – in the first and second degree, the third it is '**All these points**'

'Great and' *Solemn Obligation*; – Only the first degree has a 'Great and' Solemn Obligation, the other two are simply 'Solemn Obligations'

The Obligation of the Second Degree.
Name

WM-second   *I, ….. in the presence of/ the* Grand Geometrician of the Universe/*and of this worthy/ and worshipful/Lodge of* **Fellowcraft Freemasons**,/*regularly* **held**,/*assembled,/ and properly dedicated,/of* *my own free will and accord,/ do hereby and hereon/* **solemnly** *promise and swear/ that I will always hele,/ conceal,/ and never improperly reveal//*

The Secret

any or either/ of the secrets/ or mysteries/ of or belonging to/ the **Second Degree in Freemasonry**,/ denominated the Fellowcraft's,// to him who is but an E.A.,/ anymore than I would either of them,/ to the uninstructed/ or popular world/ who are not Masons.//

Small Print

I further solemnly **promise**/ to act as a true/ and faithful/ Craftsman,/ answer signs,/ obey summonses,/ and maintain the principles,/ inculcated in the former Degree;//

The Pledge

These **several** *points/ I solemnly swear to observe/ without evasion,/ equivocation,/ or mental reservation of any kind,//*

So help me, **Almighty** *God,/ and keep me steadfast,/ in this my solemn Obligation/ of a Fellowcraft Freemason.*

The Third Degree Obligation.

Name

WM-third   I, …………*in the presence of the* **Most High**,/ *and of this worthy* and *worshipful Lodge/ of*

Master Masons,/ duly constituted,/ *regularly assembled/ and properly dedicated,/ of my own free will and accord,/ do hereby and hereon/* **most** *solemnly promise/ and swear/ that I will always hele,/ conceal,/ and never reveal//*

The Secret

any **or either/** *of the secrets or mysteries/ of or belonging to/ the* Degree of a Master Mason//to anyone in the world,/ unless it be/ to him or them/ to whom the same/ may justly/ and lawfully belong,/ and not even to him or them/ until after due trial,/ strict examination,/ or full conviction/ that he or they/ are worthy of that confidence,/ or in the body/ of a Master Mason's Lodge/ duly opened on the Centre.//

Small Print

(I further solemnly **pledge** myself; order of phrase = **PE** Physical Education)

I further solemnly **pledge** myself/ to adhere to the principles/ of the Square and Compass,/ answer and obey/ all lawful Signs,/ and summonses/ sent to me from a Master Mason's Lodge,/ if within the length of my cable tow,/ and plead no excuse,/ except sickness/ or the pressing emergencies/ of my own **public/ or private** avocations.// (public before private duty)

Five Points of Fellowship

(I further solemnly **engage** myself; order of phrase = PE Physical Education)

I further solemnly **engage** myself/ to maintain and uphold/ the **Five Points of Fellowship**/ in act as well as in word://

Hand

that my hand,/ given to a Master Mason,/ shall be a **sure pledge**/ of **brotherhood**;//

Feet

that my feet/ shall travel **through dangers**/ and **difficulties**/ to unite with his/ in forming a column/ of **mutual defence and support**;//

Knee

that the **posture**/ of my **daily supplications**/ shall remind me of his **wants**,/ and **dispose my heart**/ to **succour his weakness**/ and **relieve his necessities**,/ so far as may-fairly be done/ without detriment/ to myself or connections;//

Breast

that my breast/ shall be the **sacred repository**/ of his secrets/ when entrusted to my care/ **murder**,/ **treason**,/ **felony**,/ and all other offences/ **contrary to the laws of God**/ and the **ordinances of the realm**/ being at all

Masonic Mnemonics

times/ most **especially excepted**.//

Honour

And finally,/ that I will maintain/ a **Master Mason's honour**/ and **carefully preserve**/ it **as my own**:/ I will not injure him myself/ or knowingly suffer /it to be done by others/ if in my power to prevent it,/ but, on the contrary,/ will **boldly repel**/ the slanderer/ of his good name,/ and most **strictly respect**/ the chastity/ of those nearest and dearest to him,/ in the persons of/ **his wife,**/ **his sister**/ **and his child**.// (I am ashamed to tell you that I remember those nearest and dearest, as it was pointed out to me that his Mother was fair game)

The Pledge

All *these points*/ *I solemnly swear to observe,*/ *without.* *evasion,*/ *equivocation*/ *or mental reservation of any kind.*//

So help me the Most High,/ *and keep me steadfast*/ *in this my solemn Obligation*/ of a Master Mason.//

A Pledge of your Fidelity

WM-first　　What you have repeated may be considered but as **a serious promise**; *as a pledge of your Fidelity, and to render* **it** *a Solemn Obligation, you will seal it with your lips on the V.S.L.* which lies before you.

First and second degree swap around the phrase 'a serious promise' and 'solemn obligation'

WM-second	*As a pledge of your fidelity, and to render* **this** *a Solemn Obligation* which might otherwise be considered but **a serious promise,** *you will seal it with your lips* **twice,** *on the V.S.L.*
WM-third	*As a pledge of your fidelity, and to render* **this binding as** *a Solemn Obligation so long as you shall live, you will seal it with your lips* **thrice** *on the V.S.L.*

Progress in Masonry

WM-second	Your progress in Masonry is marked by *the position of the Square and Compass. When you were made an E.A. both points were hid; in* **this Degree** *one* **is** *disclosed,* implying that you are now midway in Freemasonry, superior to an E.A, but inferior to that to which I trust you will hereafter attain.
WM-second	*Rise newly obligated* Fellowcraft Freemason.
WM-third	Let me once more call your attention to the *position of the Square and Compass. When you were made an E.A. both points were hid; in* **the Second Degree** *one* **was** *disclosed*; in this the whole is exhibited implying that you are now at liberty to **work with both those points** in order to render the circle of your **Masonic duties complete**.
WM-third	*Rise newly obligated Master Mason.*

First Degree Intrustment

WM-first
Having entered on the **great and** solemn Obligation of an E.A.F.M, I am now permitted to inform you that there are several Degrees in Freemasonry, with peculiar secrets restricted to each; these, however, are not **communicated** indiscriminately, but are **conferred** on Candidates according to **merit and abilities**. I shall therefore proceed to entrust you with the Secrets of this Degree, or those Marks by which we are known to each other, and distinguished from the rest of the World; but must premise for your general information that all **Squares, Levels and Perpendiculars**, are true and proper Signs to know a Mason by; you are therefore expected to **stand perfectly erect** your feet formed in a square **your body** being thus considered an **emblem of your mind**, and **your feet** of the **rectitude of your actions**.

WM-first
You will now take a short pace towards me with your left foot, bringing the right heel into its hollow; "that" is the **first** *regular step in Freemasonry, and it is in this position the Secrets of the Degree are communicated; they* *consist* *of a Sign, Grip or Token, and Word. Place your hand in this position, ...*

Second Degree Intrustment

WM-second Having taken the solemn obligation of a Fellowcraft Freemason, I shall now proceed to intrust you with the Secrets of this Degree. *You will therefore advance towards me as* **at your Initiation**. *You will now take another short pace towards me with your left foot, bringing the right heel into its hollow as before….<u>That</u> is the* **second** *regular step in Freemasonry, and it is in this position that the Secrets of the Degree are communicated. They consist,* **as in the former instance, of a Sign,** *Token, and Word,* **with this difference,** that in this Degree the Sign is of a threefold nature.

Third Degree Intrustment

WM-third I cannot better reward the attention you have paid to this exhortation and charge than by entrusting you with the secrets of the Degree. *You will therefore advance to me as* a **Fellowcraft, first as an Entered Apprentice**. *You will now take another short pace towards me with your left foot, bringing the right heel into its hollow as before. That is the* **third** *regular step in Freemasonry, and it is in this position that the secrets of the Degree are communicated. They consist* **of Signs, a Token and Word**.

Of the Signs, the first and second are casual, the third penal.

WM-first   *This,* **as you will perceive, alludes** *to the* **symbolic penalty** *of this Degree which* **implied** *that, as a man of honour,* an E.A.F.M. *would rather have* **had** .... *than improperly disclose the Secrets entrusted to him.*

WM-second   *This* **is in allusion** *to the symbolic penalty at* **one time included in the Obligation of this degree, implying** *that, as a man of honour,* a FCFM *would rather have* **had** .... *than improperly disclose the secrets entrusted to him.*

WM-third   *This* **is in allusion** *to the symbolic penalty at* **one time included in the Obligation of this degree, which implied** *that as a man of honour,* a MM *would rather have* **been** .... *than improperly disclose the secrets entrusted to him.*

First Degree Token

WM-first   *The Grip or Token is given by a distinct pressure of the ..... on the.....*

This, **when properly given and received** serves to distinguish a Brother by **night as well as by day;** *this Grip demands a Word,* a **Word highly prized amongst Masons**, as the **guard to their privileges, to much caution cannot, therefore, be observed** in communicating it; *it should never be given at length, but always by letter or syllable; to enable you to do this I must tell you what that word is:* **it is ….; please spell it after me…**

WM-first	*As during the course of the Ceremony you will be called on for this Word, the* **JD** *will now dictate the answers you are to give.*
WM-first	*What is this?*
WM-first	*What does this Grip demand?*
WM-first	*Give me that Word.*
WM-first	*Letter it and I will begin… ….*
WM-first	*This word is derived from the ……. which stood at the porch way or entrance to King Solomon's Temple, so named after …., the great ……………….., a Prince and Ruler in Israel; the import of the Word is "in ….."* Pass …

Second Degree Token

WM-first	*The Grip or Token is given by a distinct pressure of the ….. on the…..*

This Grip demands a Word, a **Word to be given with the same strict caution** as that in the **former Degree**; that is to *say it should never be given at length, but always by letter or syllable; to enable you to do this, I must tell you that the Word* *is .....; please spell it after me ....*

WM-second *As in the course of the Ceremony you will be called on for this Word, the **SD** will now dictate the answers you are to give.*

WM-second *What is this?*

WM-second *What does this Grip demand?*

WM-second *Give me that Word.*

WM-second *Letter it and I will begin; ....*

WM-second *This word is derived from the .... which stood at the porch way or entrance to King Solomon's Temple, so named after ...., the assistant High Priest, who officiated at its dedication; the import of the Word is to .... and when conjoined with that in the former Degree, ..., for God said, In .... I will ...... this mine House to stand firm forever. Pass ....*

The First and Second Degree signs are separate and distinct. The exchange between the Candidate, Masters and Wardens follow a predictable path.

Personal Comforts

WM-first *You are now at liberty to retire, in order to restore yourself to your personal comforts, and on your return to the Lodge I shall **direct** your attention to a Charge to be*

                    given by the SW, founded on the excellence
                    of our Institution and the qualifications
                    of its members. And may I be the first to
                    congratulate you on taking your first regular
                    step in Freemasonry.

WM-second   *You are now at liberty to retire, in order to
                restore yourself to your personal comforts, and
                on your return to the Lodge* I shall **call** your
                attention to a Charge/Explanation of the
                Tracing Board. And may I be the first to
                congratulate you on taking your second
                regular step in Freemasonry.

WM-third   *You are now at liberty to retire, in order to
                restore yourself to your personal comforts,
                and on your return to the Lodge* the signs,
                token and word will be further explained.

WM Brethren, I claim you attention while the — delivers
the Charge/Explanation of the Tracing Board/Traditional
History.

Distinguishing Badge

WM-first   Bro. SW, *I delegate you* **the important duty
                of investing our newly made Brother** *with
                the distinguishing badge of* **an E.A.F.M.**

WM-second & third
                Bro SW, *I delegate you to invest him with the
                distinguishing badge of a* **F.C. FM/M.M.**

Masonic Mnemonics

WM-first — <u>Let me add</u> to the observations of the SW, that you are never to put on that badge, should be about to visit a Lodge wherein there is a Brother with whom you are at **variance**, or against whom you **entertain animosity**; in such a case, it is expected you will **invite him to withdraw**, in order amicably to **settle your differences**, which if happily effected, you may then **clothe, enter the Lodge**, and work with that **love and harmony** which should at all times characterise Freemasons. But if, unfortunately, your differences are of such a nature as not to be so **easily adjusted**, it were better that one or both of you retire, than that the **harmony** of the Lodge should be **disturbed by your presence**.

WM-second — <u>Let me add to</u> what has been **stated** by the SW, that the Badge with which you have just been invested **points out to you that, as a Craftsman**, you are expected to make the **Liberal Arts and Sciences your future study**, that you may the better be enabled to discharge your duties as a Mason, and estimate the wonderful works of the Almighty.

WM-third — <u>I must state</u> that the badge with which you have now been invested not only **points out**

your rank as a Master Mason, but is meant to remind you of those great duties you have just **solemnly engaged to observe**; and whilst it marks your own superiority, it calls on you to **afford assistance and instruction** to the brethren in the inferior degrees.

The SE part of the Lodge

WM-second Masonry being a progressive science, when you were made an E. A. you were placed at the N.E. part of the Lodge to show that you were **newly admitted**. You are now placed at the S.E. part, to **mark the progress you have made in the science**. You now stand to all external appearance a **Just and Upright F.C. Freemason**, and I give it to you in strong terms of recommendation ever to continue and act as such, and as I trust the **import of the former Charge** neither is, nor ever will be effaced from your memory, I shall content myself with observing, that as in the Former Degree you made yourself **acquainted with the principles of moral truth and virtue**, you are now permitted to extend your researches **into the hidden mysteries of nature and science**.

The Exhortation

WM: Having entered upon the Solemn Obligation of a Master Mason, you are now entitled to demand that **last and greatest trial** by which alone you Candidate be admitted to a participation of the secrets of this Degree;//

Retrospect

but it is first my duty to call your attention to a retrospect of those degrees in Freemasonry through which you have already passed, that you may the better be *enabled to distinguish and appreciate the connection of our whole system*, and the *relative dependency* of its several parts.

Birth

Your admission among Masons in a state of **helpless indigence** was an **emblematical representation** of the entrance of all men on this, **their mortal existence**. It inculcated the useful lessons of **natural equality and mutual dependence**; it instructed you in the **active principles of universal beneficence and charity**, to seek the solace of your own distress by extending **relief and consolation** to your fellow-creatures in the hour of their affliction.

Bend to the Will of the GAU

Above all, it taught you to bend with **humility and resignation** to the will of the Great Architect of the Universe; to dedicate your heart, thus purified from every **baneful and malignant passion**, fitted only for the reception of **truth and wisdom**, to His glory and the **welfare of your fellow-mortals**.

Second Degree

Proceeding onwards, still guiding your progress by the **principles of moral truth**, you were led in the Second Degree to contemplate the **intellectual faculty** and to trace it from its **development, through the paths of heavenly science**, even to the **throne of God Himself**. The secrets of Nature and the principles of intellectual truth were then unveiled to your view.

One More Lesson

To your mind, thus modelled by **virtue and science**, Nature, however, presents one great and useful lesson more. She prepares you, **by contemplation, for the closing hour of existence**; and when by means of that contemplation she has conducted you through the **intricate windings of this mortal life**, she finally instructs you how to die.

Objects of the Third Degree

Such, my Brother, are the **peculiar objects of the Third Degree in Freemasonry**: They invite you to **reflect** on this awful subject; and teach you to feel that, to the **just and virtuous man**, death has no terrors equal to the **stain of falsehood and dishonour**.

Hiram Abiff

Of this great truth the annals of Masonry afford a glorious example in the **unshaken fidelity and noble death** of our Master Hiram Abiff, who was slain just before the

completion of King Solomon's Temple, at the construction of which he was, as no doubt you are well aware, **the principal Architect**. The manner of his death was as follows. Brother Wardens.

Conspiracy

WM: Fifteen Fellow Crafts, of that **superior class appointed to preside over the rest**, finding that the work was nearly completed and that they were not in possession of the secrets of the Third Degree, conspired to obtain them by any means, even to have **recourse to violence**.

More Determined

At the moment, however, of **carrying their conspiracy into execution**, twelve of the fifteen recanted; but three, of a more **determined and atrocious character** than the rest, persisted in their impious design, in the prosecution of which they planted themselves respectively at the **East, North, and South entrances of the Temple**, whither our Master had retired to pay his adoration to the Most High, as was his wonted custom at the hour of high twelve. (The order for this as you stand there it is a triangle with yourself, East; the Secretary North and JW is in the South. The SW is the only one out of place as he is in the Secretary place, link the S. This is an unusual configuration as it moves round the Lodge against the Sun)

74   *Masonic Mnemonics*

Three Ruffians (**OAP** Old Age Pensioner = **O**pposed, **A**ccosted and **P**osted)

Having finished his devotions, he attempted to return by the **South** entrance, where he was **opposed** by the first of those ruffians, who, **for want of other weapon**, had armed himself with a **heavy Plumb Rule**, and in a threatening manner demanded the secrets of a Master Mason, warning him that death would be the consequence of a refusal. Our Master, true to his Obligation, answered that those secrets were known to **but three in the world** and that without the consent and **co-operation of the other two** he neither could nor would divulge them, but intimated that he had no doubt **patience and industry would, in due time**, entitle the worthy Mason to a participation of them, but that, for his own part, he would **rather suffer death than betray the sacred trust reposed in him**. (South, North then East. It moves round the Lodge as the Sun moves) (SOAP is another key that is commonly used to help with the first entrance of the temple, South then Opposed, Accosted and Posted)

This answer not proving satisfactory, the ruffian aimed a violent blow at the head of our Master; but being startled at the firmness of his demeanour, it missed his forehead and only glanced on his **right temple** but with such force as to cause him to reel and sink on his **left knee**. (Plumb **Rule**, link **R**ule with **R**ight temple and it's down on his Left knee)

(The next two answers are very similar; I remember the order by 'Give and Receive' 'Firmness against insolent demands' this triggers off the lines; <u>he gave</u>; <u>with undimin-</u>

ished firmness; and in the next section, who received; insolent demand; firm and unshaken)

Recovering from the shock he made for the **North** entrance where he was **accosted** by the second of those ruffians, to whom he gave a **similar answer** with undiminished firmness, when the ruffian, who was armed with a **Level** struck him a violent blow on the **left temple** which brought him to the ground on his **right** knee. (Level, link with Left Temple and it's down on the right knee)

Knock Down

Finding his retreat cut off at both those points, **he staggered, faint and bleeding**, to the **East** entrance where the third ruffian was **posted**, who received a **similar answer** to his insolent demand, for even at this trying moment our Master remained firm and unshaken, when the **villain**, who was armed with a **heavy Maul**, struck him a violent blow on the forehead; which laid him lifeless at his feet. (All ruffians until the last one who was a villain)

Sacred Trust

The Brethren will take notice that in the **recent ceremony**, as well as in his **present situation**, our Brother has been made to represent one of the brightest characters recorded in the annals of Masonry, namely Hiram Abiff, who lost his life in **consequence** of his **unshaken fidelity** to the **sacred trust reposed in him**, and I hope this will make a lasting impression on his and your minds should you ever be placed in a similar state of trial.

Brother **Junior Warden**, you will endeavour to raise the representative of our Master by the **Entered Apprentice's Grip**.

JW: Worshipful Master, it proves a slip.

Brother **Senior Warden**, you will try the **Fellow Craft's**.

SW: Worshipful Master, it proves a slip likewise.

Brother Wardens, having both failed in your attempts, there remains a third method, by taking a more **firm hold of the sinews of the hand** and raising by the **Five Points of Fellowship**, which with your assistance, I will make trial of.
   It is thus all **Master Masons are raised from a figurative grave** to a reunion with the former companions of their toils. Brother Wardens, resume your seats.

The Charge (This is in my view a piece of high drama and one of the most poignant pieces of the ceremony. I make sure that I do not hurry this and keep eye contact with the candidate throughout. Thus when I focus on an object his eyes follow mine).

Want of Light

Let me now beg you to **observe that the Light** of a Master Mason is **darkness visible**, serving only to express that **gloom** which rests on the **prospect of futurity**. It is that **mysterious veil** which the **eye of human reason cannot**

penetrate, unless assisted by that **Light which is from above**.

Inevitable Destiny

Yet, even by **this glimmering ray**, you may perceive that you stand on the **very brink of the grave** into which you have just **figuratively descended**, and which, when this **transitory life shall have passed away**, will again **receive** you into its **cold bosom**. Let the **emblems of mortality** which lie before you **lead you to contemplate**, on your **inevitable destiny**, and guide **your reflections** to that most interesting of all human studies, the **knowledge of yourself**.

Time

Be careful to **perform your allotted task** while it is **yet day**. Continue to listen to the **voice of Nature**, which bears **witness** that even in this **perishable frame** resides a **vital and immortal principle**, which inspires a **holy confidence** that the **Lord of Life** will enable us to **trample** the **King of Terrors beneath our feet**, and **lift our eyes** to that **bright Morning Star**, whose rising brings **peace and salvation** to the **faithful and obedient** of the human race.

Secrets of the Degree

I cannot better reward the attention you have paid to this exhortation and charge than *by entrusting you with the secrets of the Degree. You will therefore advance to me as a*

*Fellowcraft, first as an Entered Apprentice. You will now take another short pace towards me with your left foot, bringing the right heel into its hollow as before. That is the **third** regular step in Freemasonry, and it is in this position that the secrets of the Degree are communicated. They consist of Signs, a Token and Word.*

Of the Signs, **the first and second are casual, the third penal**. The first casual Sign is called the Sign of Horror, and is given from the Fellow Crafts. Stand to order as a Fellow Craft by..............................particularly Master Masons.

The Grip or Token is the first of the Five Points of Fellowship. They are hand to hand, foot to foot, knee to knee, breast to breast and hand over back and may be thus briefly explained.
Hand to hand, I greet you as a Brother;
foot to foot, I will support you in all your laudable undertakings;
knee to knee the posture of my daily supplications shall remind me of your wants; breast to breast, your lawful secrets when entrusted to me as such I will keep as my own; and hand over back, I will support your character in your absence as in your presence.

It is in this position, and this only, and then only in a whisper, except in open Lodge, that the word is given: it is ....or ....
This runs much the same as the other degrees, just the

order of the three signs to remember. The development of the signs are not for discussion here but do not usually cause a problem. Although I hear regular debates on how they should be done properly! The five points of fellowship are the same as are used throughout the degree, with one small difference that seems to cause many a problem.

From the obligation: That my breast shall be the **sacred repository** of his secrets when entrusted to my care; becomes; your **lawful secrets** when entrusted to me as such I will keep as my own.

The Independent Magazine for Freemasons

the SQUARE

Now produced in a high quality A4 glossy format
The Square is an indispensable magazine for all Freemasons.

Produced quarterly in March, June, September and December it provides illuminating articles of a general nature on all manner of Masonic topics - news and views from home and overseas, book reviews, guidance, history plus much, much more!

REMEMBER - subscribe to *The Square* and receive a
NEW SQUARE LOYALTY CARD which entitles holders to all the following benefits:

10% discount on (defined) Toyes Regalia and Books!
10% discount on Masonic books through Lewis Masonic!
10% discount on all Ian Allan Book & Model Shop purchases!
10% discount on subscriptions to all other Ian Allan magazines!

Price: £2.95
I year subscription:
UK £11.80 /Europe £13.80 / All other areas £15.30

For all subscription details please contact:
The Square Subscriptions • Ian Allan Publishing Ltd • Riverdene Business Park • Molesey Road • Hersham • Surrey • KT12 4RG
Tel: 01932 266622 • Fax: 01932 266633
e-mail: subs@ianallanpublishing.co.uk

Lewis Masonic